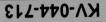

HOOKWELL'S SCHOOL

Captain Hookwell

(and Blackbeak)

Mr Mallick

Colin Bootleg

Josh Cutler

Carlos Fernandez

Erin Flint

Han Hopkins

Amber Stormbrow

Chapter 1

Josh Cutler was enjoying his first term at Hookwell's School. It was the top school for the children of pirates. But Josh had a problem. His mum wasn't a pirate – she was a pilot. If Captain Hookwell, the head teacher, ever found out, he would be expelled. Only his friends Carlos, Amber and Han knew his secret.

"Ahoy shipmates," boomed Captain Hookwell, in morning assembly. Her parrot, Blackbeak, was perched on her hat.

"Ahoy Captain," called the pupils.

"Hookwell's School is running out of money," she said. "We can't have our pirate party this term."

The pirates groaned.

HOOKWELL'S SCHOOL
FOR PROPER
PIRATES
3

Written by Jan Burchett and Sara Vogler
Illustrated by Jack Viant

RISING★STARS

Hachette UK's policy is to use papers that are natural, renewable and recyclable products and made from wood grown in well-managed forests and other controlled sources. The logging and manufacturing processes are expected to conform to the environmental regulations of the country of origin.

ISBN: 9781398325395
Text © 2021 Jan Burchett and Sara Vogler
Illustrations, design and layout © Hodder and Stoughton Ltd

First published in 2021 by Hodder & Stoughton Limited (for its Rising Stars imprint, part of the Hodder Education Group), An Hachette UK Company, Carmelite House, 50 Victoria Embankment, London EC4Y 0DZ
www.risingstars-uk.com

Impression number 10 9 8 7 6 5 4 3 2 1
Year 2025 2024 2023 2022 2021

Author: Jan Burchett and Sara Vogler
Series Editor: Tony Bradman
Commissioning Editor: Hamish Baxter
Illustrator: Jack Viant/Bright Group International
Educational Reviewer: Helen Marron
Design concept and page layout: Gary Kilpatrick
Editor: Amy Tyrer

With thanks to the schools that took part in the development of Reading Planet KS2, including: Ancaster CE Primary School, Ancaster; Downsway Primary School, Reading; Ferry Lane Primary School, London; Foxborough Primary School, Slough; Griffin Park Primary School, Blackburn; St Barnabas CE First & Middle School, Pershore; Tranmoor Primary School, Doncaster; and Wilton CE Primary School, Wilton.

A catalogue record for this title is available from the British Library.

Printed in the United Kingdom.

Orders: Please contact Hachette UK Distribution, Hely Hutchinson Centre, Milton Road, Didcot, Oxfordshire, OX11 7HH.
Telephone: (44) 01235 400555. Email: primary@hachette.co.uk.

MIX
Paper from
responsible sources
FSC™ C104740
FSC
www.fsc.org

"And Blackbeak will have to eat cheap bird seed," she added sadly.

Blackbeak squawked.

Captain Hookwell sighed. "I hope we'll find treasure soon, shipmates."

"Will the school have to close?" Josh asked his friends as they trooped out of assembly.

"Not if we can help it!" said Amber.

Josh hated to think that Hookwell's School might have to close. He loved his pirate lessons, even if he wasn't very good at them yet. He loved rowing on the sea and learning to use a spyglass and sleeping in a hammock.

They went to the post cabin to fetch their letters.

Josh's mum had sent a postcard from Trinidad.

Suddenly someone snatched it from his hand. It was Erin. Her friend, Colin, was lurking behind her. Josh had stood up to Erin once and she'd never forgiven him.

"Every day you get a postcard from a different part of the world," she said. "How can your mother sail so quickly? It's impossible!"

"She's got an extra-speedy ship," said Josh.

"There's something fishy going on here," said Erin. "And I'm going to find out what it is."

She stalked off, smirking. Colin scampered after her.

"Do you think she knows Mum isn't a pirate?" Josh asked his friends.

"No," said Amber. "Erin is just a windbag."

Josh hoped Amber was right.

Amber opened her post.

"It's a treasure map from my uncle, Sleepy Stormbrow!" she cried.

It showed a rocky island with a red X in the middle.

"That's where the treasure will be," said Han.

"Why didn't your uncle use the map himself, Amber?" asked Carlos.

"He's always asleep!" chuckled Amber. "Let's find this treasure and give it to Captain Hookwell as a surprise."

Josh felt himself bubble with excitement.

"We'll be able to have our party."

Something stirred behind a tree. They heard footsteps scuttle away.

"Who is that?" cried Josh, pointing to a girl running down the road.

"She's wearing the Grabbit School uniform," said Carlos.

"She must be a spy for Captain Squint," said Han.

Captain Squint was the head teacher of Grabbit School for Pirates. He was Captain Hookwell's sworn enemy and he was always up to no good.

"I bet that girl heard us talking about the map," said Josh.

"And now she will tell Squint all about it," said Amber angrily.

Chapter 2

"Captain Squint can't do anything without the map," said Carlos.

"He'd better not try," growled Amber.

They walked off to their class cabin and sat in a huddle.

"Let's make our treasure hunt plans before our first lesson," whispered Han.

Amber laid out the map. "I'll be leader," she said firmly. "My family are expert map readers."

"What about your great-great-great-grandad Sneezy Stormbrow?" scoffed Carlos. "He ended up in a tree with a bear!"

"Did the bear eat him?" asked Josh.

"No," said Amber. "He sneezed it out of the tree!"

They looked at the map.

Han scratched her head. "Where could that island be?" she said.

Mr Mallick, their teacher, came in. He spotted the parchment before Amber could hide it. He walked over to their bench.

"What have you got there, Amber?" he said.

"A treasure map, sir," muttered Amber.

"Treasure!" exclaimed Mr Mallick. "Just what the school needs." He studied the map.

"That's Skull Island," he said. "It's north-north-east of here. We'll all set sail at dawn to find it!"

"But it's my map," said Amber.

"Shipmates always share their treasure maps," said Mr Mallick, sternly.

"He's right," whispered Carlos. "Pirate Code number thirty-three."

Amber folded up her map. "I wanted it to be our secret adventure," she whispered back.

That night as Josh slept, a ball of seaweed whizzed through the air and hit him on the nose. He tried to sit up and fell out of his hammock.

"Josh, Carlos, over here!" Amber and Han were outside the cabin porthole. They were holding balls of seaweed.

Josh woke Carlos.

"My map's been snatched from under my hammock," said Amber, "and I know who took it." She held up a large brown bird feather.

"Scar!" whispered Carlos. "Captain Squint's pet eagle."

"We saw Squint's ship sailing away," said Han. "He's going to get our treasure!"

"Not if we get our map back first," said Josh.

"But we don't know which way to go," whispered Amber.

"We do," said Carlos. "Mr Mallick said Skull Island is north-north-east."

"Then what are we waiting for?" said Han. "Meet you at the jetty!"

Chapter 3

Josh and Carlos hurtled down to the school jetty to meet the girls.

They jumped on to the school mini-galleon. It was the first time Josh had been on a sailing ship. He hoped he wouldn't let his friends down. They'd been sailing ships since they were in their pirate prams.

Han took the wheel. "Pull up the anchor," she called. "Stay alert, shipmates."

Amber and Josh heaved on the rope to pull up the anchor. Then Amber showed Josh how to hoist the sails.

The ship began to glide through the waves.

"Come on, Josh," said Amber. "We need to trim the sails. I'll show you how."

She pulled on a rope to make the sails catch the wind.

Josh helped. Pulling on ropes in the school hall was easier – the school didn't rock!

At that moment, the galleon started to pitch and toss wildly.

"The topsail's come loose," cried Amber.

"Go up and fix that sail, Josh," called Carlos. Josh froze. A proper pirate would be up the rigging and fixing the topsail before you could say sea cucumber! But he hadn't told his friends that he was scared of going up high.

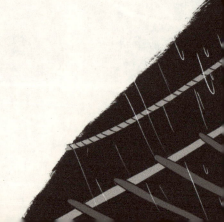

"Hurry!" yelled Han. She was having a battle with the wheel while Amber and Carlos struggled with the other sails.

It was up to Josh. The knotted ropes of the rigging towered over him. He gritted his teeth and clawed his way up.

Don't fall, he thought as he clung to the slippery ropes.

The strong wind pulled at him. He clutched the rigging tightly.

Josh reached for the flapping topsail and nearly lost his grip.

The sea swirled far below. Fighting the wind, he pulled the sail close and clutched its loose rope. He tied it tightly with a reef knot – the only knot he knew. But it did the trick. The ship glided through the water again.

Josh looked across the moonlit sea. He saw a rock shaped like a massive skull looming out of the darkness.

"Skull Island, ahoy," he yelled.

A tatty ship with patched sails was anchored in the bay. It was Squint's ship and it was empty.

Chapter 4

The friends anchored the galleon behind the skull-shaped rock. They took spades and compasses and rowed to the beach in a small boat.

Carlos held a lantern. It lit up a trail of footprints.

"They went this way," he said.

"I smell cooking," said Josh.

"Then the enemy must be close," said Han.

They came to a clearing and ducked behind some ferns. Carlos put out the lantern. Squint's pupils were huddled over a frying pan which sizzled on a fire.

Squint sat with his feet up, clutching the map. Scar, his eagle, stalked around the clearing.

"Hurry up with my grub," bellowed Squint.

"But what about finding the treasure?" said a girl.

"Plenty of time," said Squint. "Those squirmy little Hookwell kids won't be coming after us. They haven't got the map!"

"Grub's up!" called a pupil.

Squint tossed the map down and went to sit by the fire to eat. Scar swooped and snatched the map in her beak. She perched on a tree, looking round with her beady eyes.

"I'll throw a sack over Scar," whispered Amber.

"You'll have a sack full of angry eagle," said Carlos. "And anyway, we don't have a sack!"

Josh was watching Scar. The eagle had her eye on Squint's food. She ruffled her feathers angrily.

"She's hungry," said Josh. "If we feed her, she'll let go of the map."

"It might work," said Carlos.

"The trees are full of nuts," said Han.

"Do eagles eat nuts?" asked Amber.

"She looks so hungry she'll eat anything," said Josh.

Josh picked some nuts and rolled them along the ground.

Scar looked at the nuts rolling by. But she didn't drop the map.

"I'll try again," said Josh. He took a big handful of nuts and tossed them into the nettles on the other side of the clearing. Scar dropped the map and dived after them.

Josh started to crawl over to the map.

Suddenly Squint stood up. "Scar, fetch my map," he said, rubbing his belly. "I'm full. Just right for a treasure hunt."

But the eagle didn't appear.

"Where's that bird?" said Squint, turning round to find her.

Josh froze. Squint was going to see him!

Chapter 5

"What about us?" moaned Squint's pupils. "We're hungry too."

"Stop your squawking!" snapped Squint, forgetting Scar. "I haven't got any money to buy food for you. That's why we need the treasure. Get marching!"

Josh scuttled back out of sight.

The Grabbit pupils grumbled to themselves as they lined up.

"Now what are we going to do?" said Carlos.

Josh remembered something he'd seen in a film.

"Hide all around the clearing and copy me," he said.

"I'm too hungry to hunt for treasure," he called out, trying to sound like a Grabbit pupil.

"Give me food!" called Carlos.

"Who said that?" bellowed Squint.

"We want grub," called Amber.

The Grabbit pupils joined in, thinking that their shipmates were being brave. "GRUB!" they yelled, crowding round Squint.

Josh crawled over and snatched up the map. Scar screeched out of the nettles. Josh scrambled away as the angry bird swooped. He felt her claws scratch him through his shirt but he held on tightly to the map.

Han appeared, waving her spade at the eagle.

Scar flew off. The four friends crept away, being careful not to leave a trail for Squint to follow.

"You made them mutiny, Josh!" said Amber.

"What's a mutiny?" asked Josh.

"It's when the crew won't do what the captain says," explained Carlos.

Carlos lit the candle in the lantern and they huddled round the map.

"We go north-east," said Amber, checking her compass. "Through the forest to the stream."

"We must hurry," said Josh. "Squint will soon find he's lost the map and come looking for it."

They came to a riverbank. The water thundered along at their feet. It swirled over jagged rocks.

"This isn't a stream," said Carlos. "It's a wide river. You didn't read the map properly, Amber."

"I did," insisted Amber. "It must have rained a lot."

"Is it safe to use the rocks to cross?" asked Josh.

"It's the only way," said Carlos. He held up his lantern and set off.

Josh followed on to the slippery rocks.

Suddenly Carlos lost his footing.

Chapter 6

Josh grabbed Carlos by his belt. They wobbled on the slippery stones. If they fell in, they would be swept away. He gave a tug and Carlos found his footing.

"Thanks, Josh," he said when they reached the bank.

When they were all across, Amber looked at the map. "We turn west when we get to that tree," she said, pointing to a tall fir tree lit by the moon.

As they got to the fir, Josh heard a spooky cry.

"Something's stalking us," he said.

His friends stopped and waited. The night was silent again.

Amber checked her compass. "This way," she said.

"Stop!" cried Han, leaping back.

Carlos held up the lantern. A long wide crack in the ground lay before them. There was no way round. "Your map's useless, Amber," he said.

"It isn't!" said Amber. "There must have been an earthquake since it was drawn. Look at all the fallen trees."

"How do we get across?" asked Josh.

"We swing," said Han, pulling at a creeper on a tree. "This is strong."

"Is it safe?" said Josh.

"It'll be like swinging on the rigging at school," said Han.

She took a run up, clutched the creeper and swung to the other side. She let the creeper swing back. Amber and Carlos followed. Now it was Josh's turn.

He looked down into the big drop underneath. *I don't think I can do this,* he thought.

Josh heard a sound behind him but he didn't wait to find out what it was. Clutching the creeper, he ran and jumped. As he swung across the gap, he glimpsed the deep, dark drop below ... and then he landed on the other side, but right on the edge. He was falling back! Carlos shot out a hand and saved him.

27

"One good turn deserves another!" said Carlos, grinning. "Number thirty-seven in the Pirate Code."

Amber led them to a clearing. She read some words on the map. "Turn south at the lightning tree and walk thirteen paces."

Carlos held up the lantern and they searched the clearing.

Josh saw a blackened, twisted tree.

"Found it," he called.

Amber walked to the tree, checked her compass and walked thirteen paces south.

"Now I turn to the crocodile and walk two paces," she said.

"Crocodile?" exclaimed Josh in alarm.

"Not a real one," said Amber.

Han took the lantern and held it over a long, low rock. It had a little hole that looked like a beady eye.

"That's the crocodile!" she said.

Amber walked two steps. "Now we dig!"

They started to dig in the soft ground.

There was an awful screech overhead. An eagle flapped away.

"That's Scar," said Carlos. "She'll lead the enemy here."

Suddenly, Han's spade rattled against something hard. They scrabbled at the soil. A wooden chest appeared.

29

Josh thought he would burst with excitement. They'd found the treasure!

Amber opened the chest. Silver cups and gold chains and rings sparkled in the lantern light.

"We've found a fortune," said Han. "Captain Hookwell will be delighted."

"Wait," said Carlos, "I have to tell you something about this treasure."

"Tell us later," said Amber. "We need to get this back to our ship."

But it was too late. At that moment Squint's pirates burst into the clearing.

Chapter 7

The friends were held prisoner on Squint's ship. It was dark and smelly and their hands were tied behind them. Josh squirmed and pulled at his ropes. He had a plan.

"It wasn't a fair fight," moaned Amber. "Now we're locked in a cage and Squint's got our treasure."

"We don't have to bother about the treasure," began Carlos.

"What!" shouted Amber. "But the school needs money."

Josh struggled with his ropes again.

"Let's not argue. That won't help," he said, "but this might!"

He held out his untied hands.

"How did you do that?" said Han, startled.

"It's a trick I saw in a book," explained Josh. He untied the others. "If someone is tying you up, you secretly hold your hands apart. Then when you are tied up, you have room to wiggle them free."

"That's a brilliant pirate trick," said Carlos.

"Let's get out of here," said Han. She rattled the bars.

Squint suddenly loomed out of the darkness.

"How did you get free?" he shouted. "You'll all walk the plank for this!"

Josh felt prickles of fear run down his spine.

Squint bundled them through a hatch and up on to the main deck.

He put a plank over the side. Josh felt a stab of hope. Their mini galleon was directly underneath the plank.

"But, sir," called out one of Squint's pupils. "They'll just land on their ship."

"I knew that!" said Squint quickly. He snatched up the plank and staggered to the other side with it.

Josh saw dark shapes swimming round the ship. They were sharks and they didn't look friendly.

"I'll go first," said Han.

She walked up to the plank and sprang boldly on to it. She marched right to the end.

33

Josh's mouth was dry and his hands shook. *How can Han be so brave?* he thought.

"Jump, you lily-livered cuttlefish!" bellowed Squint.

Han jumped on the end of the plank, but she didn't jump into the sea. She landed on the plank again. She sprang higher and higher.

All of a sudden, she spun in the air in an incredible backflip, sailed over their heads and landed on the deck. "Get those Grabbits!" she cried.

Chapter 8

Han cartwheeled round the deck sending Squint flying.

Josh snatched up a bucket of smelly water and threw it over the Grabbits.

Carlos rolled a barrel along the deck, bowling the enemy over like skittles.

"You won't escape," cried a boy as he tried to hit Amber with a mop. She jumped aside and the mop hit a Grabbit shipmate. They began to fight. Soon all the Grabbit pupils were in a bundle, fighting each other.

Then Josh spotted Squint clambering up the rigging.

"Who's a lily-livered cuttlefish now!" he shouted, setting off after him. Josh hadn't got far when he saw how high he was. But there was no turning back now.

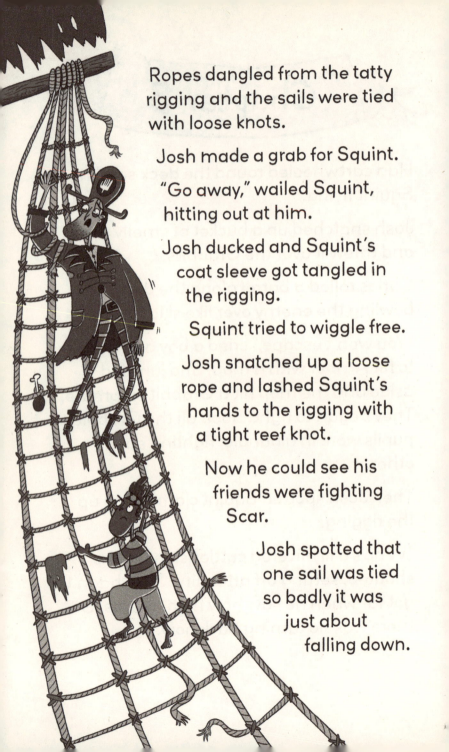

Ropes dangled from the tatty rigging and the sails were tied with loose knots.

Josh made a grab for Squint.

"Go away," wailed Squint, hitting out at him.

Josh ducked and Squint's coat sleeve got tangled in the rigging.

Squint tried to wiggle free.

Josh snatched up a loose rope and lashed Squint's hands to the rigging with a tight reef knot.

Now he could see his friends were fighting Scar.

Josh spotted that one sail was tied so badly it was just about falling down.

He pulled it free. The sail fell, trapping Scar and all the Grabbit pupils.

Josh scrambled down to the deck.

"Let's go," shouted Carlos.

"Not without our treasure," said Amber.

"The treasure chest isn't important," said Carlos frantically. "We must sail now."

"Carlos is right," said Josh.

They jumped on their ship and untied it.

"Come back, you horrible shrimps!" screamed Squint from the rigging.

When they arrived at Hookwell's School, Captain Hookwell and Blackbeak were standing on the jetty. They looked stern.

Erin and Colin stood beside them, looking smug.

"Erin tells me you didn't sleep in your hammocks," said Captain Hookwell. "Where have you been?"

They told her everything

"Squint stole our treasure," said Han.

"I've been trying to explain," said Carlos. "That treasure was rubbish ..."

"Are you saying my map was useless?" growled Amber.

"... apart from this!" Carlos pulled a shimmering pearl from his pocket. "It's called the Duke's Pearl. I read about it in my Lost Treasure book."

"Shiver me buckles!" exclaimed the captain. "Thanks to you four, we can have our party."

38

Chat about the book

1 Go to page 6. Why did Erin say, "There's something fishy going on here"?

2 Read page 22. Why did the Grabbit pupils think their shipmates were being brave?

3 Look at page 15. Why did the authors use 'clawed', 'gritted' and 'clutched' when Josh was climbing the rigging?

4 Go to Chapter 6. How did Josh, Carlos and Amber respond when they found the treasure?

5 Read the last paragraph in Chapter 8. What do you think is going to happen next? Why did the author end the story in this way?

6 Which is your favourite part of the story? Why?

Erin and Colin scowled.

Josh loved the party. Everyone high-fived him and his friends. They got first go on the inflatable galleon. They played Hook-a-Shark and threw seaweed at the teachers!

Now Josh really was a proper pirate.

Erin and Colin sidled up to him.

"Enjoy it while you can," Erin muttered. "I don't think your mum's a pirate and I'm going to find the proof. Then you'll be expelled."

"You'll be expelled," said Colin.

Josh gulped. How could he keep his secret safe? He knew one thing. He wasn't going to leave Hookwell's School without a fight.